PASSION & PAIN:

The Suffering Church Today

by
David Alton
with
Michele Lombardo

Jubilee Campaign

Copyright © Jubilee Campaign 2003

Published by Jubilee Campaign

Jubilee Campaign is a Christian-based human rights group dedicated to lobbying authorities to protect children at risk and persecuted Christians.

St Johns Cranleigh Rd, Wonersh, Guildford, Surrey, GU5 0QX, United Kingdom

All rights reserved. No part of this publication may be reproduced or transmitted by any means – electronic or mechanical – without prior permission of the publisher.

Cover Design by Maria Kaczperski - used by kind permission of Eternal Word Television Network (EWTN)

Produced and printed by Bill Gribbin, The Old Hall Press, Old Hall Green, Ware, Herts. SG11 1DU, United Kingdom.

Warning: contains graphic descriptions of real persecution not suitable for children.

ISBN: 0 9546258 0 3

CONTENTS

Introduction	i
Section One	1
Week One: The Sudan	2
Week Two: Indonesia	12
Week Three:	
The Islamic Republic of Pakistan	19
Week Four: The Arab Republic of Egypt	25
Week Five: The Islamic Republic of Iran	31
Week Six: The Kingdom of Saudi Arabia	37
Section Two	42
Week Seven: The Democratic People's	
Republic of Korea	43
Week Eight: The People's Republic of China	51
Week Nine: Vietnam	62
Week Ten: Laos	70
Section Three	78
Week Eleven: India	79
Week Twelve: Burma/Myanmar	85
Week Thirteen: Turkmenistan and the	
Successor States of the Former Soviet Union	94
Final Notes:	102

ACKNOWLEDGEMENTS

I would like to convey my special thanks to all those who have committed their time and effort to making this important book possible. I'd like to express my gratitude to my co-author Michele Lombardo who was the engine behind the writing and to all those who contributed to the 13-part TV series - The Suffering Church - broadcast by Eternal Word Television Network (EWTN). Rebecca Amos, Christina Borges and Doug Keck were especially instrumental. Many thanks also to the outstanding efforts of the Jubilee Campaign team including Danny Smith, Ann Buwalda, Karin Finkler, Melody Divine, Wilfred Wong, David Mundy, Mark Rowland, Derek Williams, Kumar Selvakumaran, Kie-Eng Go, Bonnie Ryason and Mike Morris. I would like to thank Martin Foley and Barbara Mace for their support and work on this project. Finally, thanks to my friend Bill Gribbin, who kindly agreed to print and produce this book.

David Alton

SUFFERING CHURCH VIDEOS

A 13-part set of videos - called *The Suffering Church* - is available to be used in conjunction with this book. The series reveals the persecution of Christians in the same 13 countries covered in this book and was broadcast by Eternal Word Television Network (EWTN). EWTN have kindly given permission for us to reproduce these videos at a reduced cost. The series is an excellent resource for use in small groups, seminars, lessons or churches.

For more information, please contact Jubilee Campaign UK - 00 44 1483 894 787 or email
info@jubileecampaign.co.uk

Introduction:

This thirteen-week devotional tells the stories of real live Christian believers living in some of the most rigorous and punishing of circumstances. Women and men, old and young, from all denominational backgrounds who share a common commitment to remain faithful to Jesus and his Gospel in spite of all the terrors unjust regimes might choose to throw at them. These are the heroes of the faith. The challenge is presented to us to pray with them.

As followers of Jesus Christ, it is also important to reflect on His life, death, and resurrection, and to take time to consider the tremendous sacrifice and suffering He bore on our behalf.

St. Paul tells us:

> *For I determined to know nothing among you except Jesus Christ, and Him crucified* (1 Corinthians 2:2).

In reading Holy Scripture, and through prayer, reflection, and worship, we soon come to realize the enormity of that suffering and sacrifice. The Nicene Creed recalls these things beautifully:

> *For us and for our salvation He came down from heaven. By the power of the Holy Spirit He was born of the Virgin Mary, and became man. For our sake He was crucified*

> *under Pontius Pilate; He suffered, died, and was buried. On the third day He rose again in fulfillment of the Scriptures; He ascended into heaven and is seated at the right hand of the Father. He will come again in glory to judge the living and the dead, and His kingdom will have no end.*

God the Father sacrificed His only Son so that the world could be saved through Him:

> *For God so loved the world, that He gave His only begotten Son, that whoever believes in Him should not perish, but have eternal life* (John 3:16).

Jesus was reviled, mocked, and expelled from towns where His only crime was to preach the Truth, heal the sick, and raise the dead. Misunderstood and rejected, abandoned by His own disciples, He was spat upon, and crowned with thorns. Nails were driven through His flesh as He was pinned to a cross upon which He hung until He died an agonizing death. This our Saviour did for us:

> *He Himself bore our sins in His body on the cross, that we might die to sin and live for righteousness; for by His wounds you were healed* (1 Peter 2:24).

Jesus was not alone in His suffering. He warned St. Peter that he too would suffer and die for his faith.

St Paul and countless Christians in the 1st Century Church endured unspeakable suffering and persecution. They were thrown to the lions, beheaded, and subjected to torture and gruesome death. But such atrocities are not merely part of ancient history: they continue to occur at an alarming rate. Since St. Stephen became the first Christian martyr, millions have been persecuted for their faith, and for love of the Lord they follow. St. Peter reminds us:

> *For you have been called for this purpose, since Christ also suffered for you, leaving you an example for you to follow in His steps* (1 Peter 2:21).

The persecution of Christians today is staggering and often far graver in its breadth and severity than any suffered in history. More Christians – Catholic, Protestant and Orthodox - were martyred in the 20th Century than in the previous nineteen centuries combined. Of the world's six billion inhabitants, more than half live in countries where being a Christian could cost you your life.

In this 13-week devotional, we shall explore the plight of the persecuted and suffering Church worldwide, embarking on a country-by-country journey, wherein our eyes and our hearts will be opened to the suffering of the 21st Century Church. We begin with the persecution of Christians in the Muslim world, focusing on the countries of Sudan,

Indonesia, Pakistan, Egypt, Iran, and Saudi Arabia. Secondly, we consider the persecution of Christians under the Asian Communist regimes of North Korea, China, Vietnam, and Laos. Thirdly, we consider the persecution of Christians in India, Burma/Myanmar, and in Turkmenistan and the other successor states of the former Soviet Union. Although this list is extensive, it is not exhaustive. Christians in many additional countries are also persecuted for their faith.

It is our prayer that you the reader will set aside time each week for 13 weeks to consider the courage and suffering of your brothers and sisters throughout the world. At the end of this time, we hope you will return to the beginning, committing to prayer once again those with whom you have become so familiar. As you grow familiar with them through their stories, we hope too that you will join them in prayer and pray for them. Thank you in advance for opening your hearts, lifting your prayers, and taking action as the Lord gently leads you. It is our sincere desire that you will sense the strong thread with which we are all bound to these dear ones. As the Apostle Paul writes:

> *For just as we have many members in one body and all the members do not have the same function, so we, who are many, are one body in Christ, and individually members one of another* (Romans 12:4-5).

Before We Begin:
A Brief Introduction to
the Jubilee Campaign

The Jubilee Campaign was founded in the early 1980s in England. From its humble beginnings, its founder and UK Director, Danny Smith, sought to establish a non-denominational and non-sectarian human rights organization that would advocate non-violent solutions to religious intolerance and religious discrimination throughout the world.

In 1987, Lord David Alton, then a Member of the British House of Commons, launched Jubilee in Parliament. Successive prime ministers, including Margaret Thatcher and Tony Blair have been strong supporters, and now more than 150 members of Parliament have adopted cases of religious persecution from around the globe.

In 1991, Jubilee Campaign USA was launched by Ann Buwalda, who continues to serve as its Director today. Jubilee USA lobbies Congress on behalf of those suffering religious persecution and human rights violations throughout the world. It advocates the release of prisoners of conscience, and the abolition of unjust laws and practices that impose imprisonment, execution, torture, harassment, and other forms of oppression upon religious and ethnic minorities. Like its British counterpart, it campaigns against the exploitation of children, particularly those affected by the abhorrent sex trade in Asia.

Danny Smith and Ms. Buwalda, and their Jubilee staff in both Britain and the US have travelled extensively to promote religious tolerance, engage in fact-finding missions, and testify before national and international bodies with regard to human and

Jubilee's founders – Danny Smith (left) with Lord Alton of Liverpool

religious rights and practices. Jubilee also actively promotes the rights and protection of children internationally, and provides financial support to many worthwhile programmes. As a licensed attorney, Ms. Buwalda has represented numerous refugees who have fled their countries of persecution, and has played an active role in the release of religious prisoners and other prisoners of conscience throughout the world.

The goal of the Jubilee Campaign is to provide a vital voice for those suffering in silence. We hope that these stories will provide you with insight and inspiration and that as you meditate on the Suffering Church you will feel compelled to take action through prayer and deed.

SECTION ONE:

Persecution of Christians in the Muslim World

Before the events of September 11, 2001, few people in the Western world knew much about the existence of militant Islamic extremists engaged in a jihad or "holy war" against Christians, Jews and the West, and even less were aware of the passion of their hostility. Since then, the reality of religiously motivated "terrorism" has become increasingly familiar. Unfortunately, Christians and other religious minorities throughout the Middle East, and parts of Asia and Africa, have been persecuted by Islamic governments and fundamentalist groups for years.

Week One:
The Sudan

Who shall separate us from the love of Christ? Shall tribulation, or distress, or persecution, or famine, or nakedness, or peril, or sword? Just as it is written, 'For Thy sake we are being put to death all day long; we were considered as sheep to be slaughtered.' But in all these things we overwhelmingly conquer through Him who loved us. For I am convinced that neither death, nor life, nor angels, nor principalities, nor things present, nor things to come, nor powers, nor height, nor depth, nor any other created thing, shall be able to separate us from the love of God, which is in Christ Jesus our Lord (Romans 8:35-39).

Sudan, which lies just to the south of Egypt, is Africa's largest country. The record of anti-Christian persecution there is one of the most atrocious in the world today. Religious minority rights are not protected, and Islam is the state religion, which confers second-class citizenship status on all non-Muslims. Backed by Muslim clerics, the National Islamic Front regime in Sudan's Arab and Muslim north declared a *jihad*, or "holy war" against the Christians and animists of the south in 1989. More than 2 million have died; more than 4 million are displaced, and countless others have been enslaved. Many of Sudan's suffering Christians feel isolated and forgotten.

Refugees inside Sudan are dying from hunger and thirst, as forced starvation is one of the primary tools of the Khartoum regime. Although humanitarian groups provide needed food supplies, the Government seizes the provisions and distributes them only to Muslims. When Government forces attack a Christian village, they burn down the houses, as well as the crops and any stored grain. Those villagers who are captured are killed, and those who escape have little hope for survival. They flee into the bush, where the temperature is in excess of 115 degrees, and where they have no food and only dysentery-infested water.

Cholera and other virulent diseases rage in Sudan, and already-starving children are particularly susceptible. The effects of daily aerial bombardment and the indiscriminate laying of anti-personnel landmines can be seen in the countless torn limbs and broken bodies. Christians are told that they can avoid all this misery by renouncing their faith and converting to Islam, after which Sudan's Government will happily care for them.

Sudan's military continues to decorate and promote known war criminals such as Commander Taib Musba, notorious for killing an estimated 15,000 unarmed civilian ethnic Uduk Christians. In 1986, he murdered five church leaders in front of the gathered Uduk villagers, announcing that the same would happen to all of them unless they renounced Christianity and convert to Islam. When the villagers refused to convert, Musba and his henchmen began killing unarmed men, women, and children. Some were herded at gunpoint into a hut, and then run over by a 50-ton Soviet-made tank. He herded groups of Christian villagers into another hut, and anyone who refused to renounce Jesus Christ was killed by a 3-inch nail driven into the top of the head.

In April 2001, Christians who had gathered at the All Saints Cathedral in Khartoum were attacked by riot police who threw teargas inside the church and fired bullets at the crowd, injuring many. Police then entered the church and indiscriminately arrested at least fifty-six people. A criminal court judge tried them the following day in less than an hour, refusing their request to be defended by legal counsel. They were all convicted of causing a public disturbance. Six women and three children were sentenced to 15 and 20 lashes respectively, and were flogged the following day and then released. The remaining forty-seven were sentenced to 20 lashes each and from 7 to 20 days in prison.

In June 2001, a Khartoum resident named Aladin Omer Agabani Mohammed was arrested for converting from Islam to Christianity, kept in solitary confinement and tortured. After three months, he was released on medical grounds, but was required to report daily to security forces. By the beginning of the following year, he was being harassed again, and on January 30, 2002, airport authorities refused to allow him to board a plane to Uganda to study at St. Paul's Theology Seminary because he was "an apostate abandoning Islam."

In 2002, Government authorities amputated the right hand of a southern Christian for stealing spare auto parts. In February of the same year, an 18-year-old southern Christian woman named Abok Alfa Akok was sentenced to death by stoning for having an extra-marital affair and becoming pregnant. The Vatican interceded, and her sentence was commuted: after giving birth to her child, she was given 75 lashes.

Indigenous militia and Rizegat and Bagarra tribesmen are armed and supported by the Sudanese Government. They raid villages in the Bahr al Ghazal region to loot property and livestock, and more egregiously, to take women and children as slaves. The targeted victims are Christians and practitioners of non-Muslim indigenous religions. International human rights groups have reported that women and children from Christian and other non-Muslim families are often forcibly converted to Islam after being captured and sold into slavery.

In the areas of southern Sudan where conflict still rages, children are being killed daily and women raped. Villagers in several areas of the northeast Upper Nile region report that when women are captured by Government forces, they are asked whether they are Muslim or Christian. Those who say they are Muslim are set free, while those who proclaim their Christianity are typically gang-raped by soldiers who then mutilate them and leave them to die in agony as an example to others. UNICEF reports that children are being crippled, nails put into their knees, and their Achilles' tendons deliberately cut so that they cannot run.

These Government-supported atrocities clearly constitute war crimes: Common Article 3 of the Geneva Conventions prohibit the deliberate targeting of civilians in times of war. Those responsible must be brought to account.

When the Southern resistance movement, the SPLA, liberated Torit, the scale of the destruction

The shattered remains of a home in Narus

there became apparent. The Cathedral church of Sts Peter and Paul had been desecrated, and the smaller church of Our Lady of the Assumption razed to the ground, leaving only one small wall. The foundations had been turned into a military bunker and the bricks taken to build a mosque. The town itself had been forcibly Islamicised.

The Catholic Auxiliary Bishop of Torit, Akio Johnson, is scarred by bullet-wounds from nine attempts on his life. Seventy-two bombs were dropped in three raids on his compound, obliterating his home, and destroying the primary and secondary school at which more than 200 children were being educated. He reported that many children were vomiting and crying and were deeply traumatized, commenting that the hatred in people has gone very deep. Clearly no reconciliation can begin before the Government ends its daily bombing of the area. Bishop Akio observes that Western countries continue to import oil from Sudan despite horrific human rights abuses: "of every barrel, half is full of oil and half is full of Sudanese blood".

It is scarcely credible that human rights abuses of this magnitude should have been allowed to continue with little intervention from the rest of the world. International human rights organizations, as well as the United States Congress have condemned Sudan's inhumane war against Christians, animists, and moderate Muslims as genocide. Nevertheless, Sudan's fundamentalist Muslim Government is

Bishop Akio: nine attempts have been made on his life.

treated with kid gloves by Western countries that want its oil and its co-operation in the post-September 11 "war against terrorism".

An executive order in 1997 barred American companies from doing business in Sudan, which earned $500 million in 2000 alone from its new oil industry. Though certain US lawmakers, like Sen. John McCain (Republican – Arizona), and Sen. Sam Brownback (Republican – Kansas) have called strongly for capital-market restrictions on Sudan, these are opposed by politicians and Wall Street. The Sudan Peace Act, designed to punish the Khartoum regime, requires the President to make a determinationand certify within six months of enactment, and every six months thereafter, that the Government of Sudan and the Sudan People's LiberationMovement are negotiating in good faith and negotiations should continue. Despite aerial bombing and other significant violations perpetrated by the Government, the President continues to certify the negotiations thereby avoiding further sanctions.

Since 1999, the US Secretary of State has designated Sudan a country of particular concern under the International Religious Freedom Act for particularly severe violations of religious freedom. In its report released in May 2002, the Commission determined that: "The Government of Sudan is the world's most violent abuser of religious freedom". Elliot Abrams, Chairman of the US Commission on

International Religious Freedom, sent a letter to US Secretary of State Colin Powell on 16 February 2003. In it, he recommended that in response to Sudan's atrocities, the US should "push vigorously for a resolution at this year's UNHRC session that clearly articulates the gross violations of human rights and humanitarian law committed by the Sudanese Government – including bombings of civilian targets, slavery, persecution of religious minorities, and interference with humanitarian assistance". Instead, during the April 2003 Session of the UN Human Rights Commission in Geneva, Switzerland, the Commission defeated re-authorizing the resolution which condemned human rights violations in the Sudan thereby terminating the position of the UN Special Rapporteur investigating and reporting those violations.

Prayer Points:

- Please pray for the protection and deliverance of the Christians and animists of southern Sudan, that they will be strengthened in their faith, and comforted in their suffering; that God in His mercy will spare them from further unspeakable horror, and raise up intercessors and advocates to lighten their heavy burdens.

- Please pray for an end to the bombings, the rapes, the murders, the forced starvation and disease;

the slavery, and other atrocities committed by the Islamic Government and Military of Sudan.

- Please pray that Western governments and other world leaders cease to remain silent with regard to the genocide and horrific human rights abuses in Sudan; that they have the conviction to place greater value on life, dignity, religious freedom and a sense of the justice due to all human beings.

- Please pray too that Christians throughout the world will inspire their leaders to grasp and maintain these priorities when negotiating over oil or other commodities with the leaders of brutal regimes.

Week Two: Indonesia

Blessed are those who have been persecuted for the sake of righteousness, for theirs is the kingdom of heaven. Blessed are you when men cast insults at you, and persecute you, and say all kinds of evil against you falsely, on account of Me. Rejoice, and be glad, for your reward in heaven is great, for so they persecuted the prophets who were before you (Matthew 5:10-12).

Indonesia is home to more Muslims than any country in the world. It also home to one of the most violent and militant Islamic extremist groups in the world: the Laskar Jihad, or "holy war," whose fighters include native Indonesian and outsiders including Afghans and Pakistanis. Laskar Jihad has infiltrated the provinces of West Papua and Sulawesi, both of which have large Christian communities. For three years following January 1999, in Maluku estimates of upwards of 80,000 Christians were forced to flee their homes and 1000s subjected to forced conversion rituals. In Central Sulawesi, numerous attacks have been carried out against Christians; nearly 20,000 have been forced to flee their villages.

On April 28, 2002, in the Moluccan village of Soya, a massacre led by about a dozen attackers armed with automatic rifles, grenades, and knives claimed the lives of at least twelve, including a tiny baby. Some of the victims were stabbed, some shot, and others burnt to death. Witnesses report that the callous assailants went from house to house, opening fire on whoever was at home. In addition to these brutal murders, the attackers set fire to thirty Christian homes and a Protestant church.

Laskar Jihad warriors have attacked Christian communities in West Papua and Central Sulawesi.

In August 2002, a number of Laskar Jihad attacks occurred in Poso, Central Sulawesi, Indonesia. On 5 August, eighty to one hundred assailants dressed in black, like ninjas, attacked the Christian village of Makato. Four women and one man were shot; two others were seriously injured, and seven reported missing. Many houses and a church were set on fire during the attack.

Three days later, an Italian tourist was killed and four other people were injured by Muslims who attacked a passenger bus. The following day, all Christian homes in the villages of Malei and Tongko were set on fire. Then on 11 August, five Christians were killed when the bus in which they were riding was hijacked. Four bodies were thrown from it as it drove through the streets of Kayamanya. On the same day, at least seventeen homes in the village of Rononuncu were burned to the ground.

Churches set aflame in an attempt to force Christians to leave Indonesia.

The following day, two more Christian villages in Poso were attacked by Laskar Jihad fighters dressed in black and firing automatic weapons. The villagers, powerless to fight off their attackers, were forced to flee, leaving their homes to be plundered and burnt to the ground. Hundreds of homes were destroyed, two churches burnt down, and at least five persons killed in the attacks, while at least two others were critically injured.

Similar attacks occurred throughout the remainder of August 2002 in Mayumba, Morowalyu, and Bunta Toini. Bombs exploded in Gebangrejo, Kayamanya, and Jalan Morotai Kelurahan Gebang, resulting in further deaths and destruction of property.

Three people were injured the following month when a bomb exploded at a Christian school in East Palu. In a related incident, Revd Rinaldy Damanik was arrested on false charges when he voluntarily reported to the Central Post of Indonesian National Police to provide testimony with regard to the Laskar Jihad attacks on these six villages in Poso. He was arrested on arrival as police claimed that he had always been a suspect and was thus to be detained.

The prison cell in which Revd Damanik was held during his trial.

15

Despite having failed to substantiate any charge against him, police extended his detention indefinitely because of pressure from political opportunists and religious extremists. This additional unlawful detention began on October 2, 2002, and has been marked by multiple and continued efforts to falsely establish his guilt. Despite these legal violations, Revd Rinaldy Dimanak was sentenced to three years imprisonment on charges of illegal weapons possession on 16 June 2003. In August 2003 his appeal to the High Court was denied. Jubilee Campaign will continue to work for his unconditional release.

The Laskar Jihad intends to Islamicize all Indonesia by force, changing its pluralist constitution to an Islamic one, and imposing strict Islamic *Shari'a* law as the law of the land. This strategy is already being enforced in the Christian areas of the Moluccas and Sulawesi, and is likely be imposed on West Papua soon. Forced conversion to Islam or utter annihilation is the choice facing Indonesia's Christian minority. It appears that Indonesia's Government and Military are both unwilling and unable to do anything to stop the dangerous, brutal Laskar Jihad gaining in strength and power in its war on Christians.

Although thousands of native Indonesians have been murdered at the hands of the Laskar Jihad, the international media paid little attention until the 12 October, 2002 bombing at a night club in Bali. That bombing, which bears a striking similarity to the tactics of the Laskar Jihad and its sister organization, Al Qaeda, claimed nearly 200 innocent lives.

Elliot Abrams, Chairman of the US Commission on International Religious Freedom, sent a letter to US Secretary of State Colin Powell on February 16, 2003. In it, he stated: "The Indonesian Government has not controlled its armed forces or the influx of armed groups from other islands, reportedly resulting in murder, forced mass resettlement, forced conversion to Islam, and torture". Abrams recommended that the United States open debate on the issue.

Prayer Points:

- Please pray for the protection and deliverance of Christians in Indonesia; that they will be strengthened in their faith and comforted in their suffering; that God in His mercy will spare them from further unspeakable horror, and raise up intercessors and advocates to lighten their heavy burdens.

- Please pray for an end to the bombings, the attacks, the massacres, and the destruction of homes and churches by the Laskar Jihad, other Islamic groups and the Indonesian Military; for an end to unjust arrests and imprisonment, and the release of Revd Rinaldy Damanik and other Christians who have been unjustly imprisoned.

- Please pray that Indonesia's leaders take a firm stand against the Islamic terrorists operating in their midst; that *Shari'a* law is not imposed, but that just laws and the rule of law are established and upheld in Indonesia; that the Indonesian Government, inspired by prayer and the encouragement and example of Christians throughout the world, will protect the lives and religious freedoms of its minority citizens.

Week Three: The Islamic Republic of Pakistan

We ourselves speak proudly of you among the churches of God for your perseverance and faith in the midst of all your persecutions and afflictions which you endure (2 Thessalonians 1:4).

The Islamic Republic of Pakistan is located in South Asia, and shares its borders with Iran, India, China, and Afghanistan. Partitioned from India in 1947, Pakistan emerged on the world map on the basis of "two Nation Theory." This theory was propounded on the grounds that Hindus and Muslims living in undivided India were two nations. Christians were then and remain now—at best—an ignored second class minority or—at worst—persecuted by the Muslim majority. In 1964, under pressure from fundamentalists, the Pakistani Constitution declared the new name of the country as "the Islamic Republic of Pakistan." Through this Constitution and contrary to the nation's founding, Islam became Pakistan's official state religion.

Muslims make up more than 95 percent of the population. Pakistan's small Christian minority accounts for less than 3 percent of the population. Christians are openly and officially discriminated against by Pakistan's government, being afforded far less legal, political, educational, and employment rights and protections than their Muslim counterparts.

Having been accused of blasphemy, Ayub Masih was finally released after six years on death-row.

Perhaps the gravest injustice in Pakistan's history has been the imposition of its abusive "blasphemy laws", under which anyone convicted of insulting Islam's Prophet Muhammad (PBUH) in word, deed, or symbol, must be put to death. These harsh statutes have been repeatedly used and abused by

Muslims against Christians to settle personal disputes – often costing the Christians their freedom, and sometimes their lives.

Christians in Pakistan are frequent victims of brutal acts of violence both by sections of the general Muslim populace, and often even more brutal ones by militant Islamic extremist groups. Pakistani police, known for their corruption, are both unwilling and unable to protect Christian citizens.

As the world has seen, Pakistan's small Christian minority has been subjected to especially heinous and frequent attacks since the September 11, 2001 terrorist attacks on the United States, and subsequent US military action in Afghanistan.

Just over a month after the events of September 11, Islamic extremists burst into a church service in Bahawalpur. Sixteen worshippers were gunned down in cold blood, and at least seven more severely wounded.

On March 17, 2002, during Sunday morning worship service, grenades were hurled by militants into the sanctuary of the International Protestant Church, which is located in the Capitol of Islamabad squarely in the midst of foreign embassies, including adjacent to the American Embassy. Five believers died, and 45 suffered various degrees of shrapnel injuries.

On August 5, 2002, masked gunmen firing automatic rifles stormed the campus of Murree Christian School, killing six and wounding three others. Less than one week later, three Muslim assailants hurled grenades into a crowd of women gathered at a church in the grounds of a Presbyterian hospital in Taxila. Three nurses were killed, and about twenty-five other people wounded.

A Pakistani church reduced to rubble.

Six weeks after that, Islamic militants entered the offices of a Christian charity organization in Karachi, tied a group of workers to their chairs, taped their mouths shut, and shot eight in the head at short-range, execution-style. Seven died, leaving only one survivor. Adding insult to horrific injury, police arrested and jailed this lone survivor and eyewitness to the massacre, falsely charging him as an accomplice to the murders in order to silence him.

Three young Christian girls lost their lives after two Muslims hurled grenades into a children's event on Christmas Day 2002 at a small Presbyterian chapel in Chianwali. Thirteen other children and their parents were wounded and at least three of the survivors have sustained permanent eye damage from splintered glass fragments driven into their faces by the grenade blast. Just days before, a local Muslim cleric named Mohammed Afzar had told his congregation that it was their sacred duty to kill Christians.

On that same Christmas Day, a shopping bag containing two handmade grenades and twenty shell-casings was discovered in the bushes outside the Protestant St. Thomas's Church in Islamabad.

Some militant Islamic extremists even murder their own countrymen as they seek out Christians and those they link with the United States and other Western countries for execution. As these incidents show, militant Muslims have specifically targeted women and children in their misconceived *jihad*. Their influence and power are growing and spreading at an alarming rate in Pakistan, and the Government is clearly unable to stop the rising tide. Hung out as lambs to the slaughter, Christians in Pakistan have been and continue to be massacred at alarming rates.

Prayer Points:

- Please pray for the protection and deliverance of Christians in Pakistan; that they will be strengthened in their faith and comforted in their suffering; that God in His mercy will spare them from further unspeakable horror, and raise up intercessors and advocates to lighten their heavy burdens.

- Please pray for an end to the bombings, the attacks, the massacres, the rapes, the murders, and the destruction of homes and churches by Islamic extremist groups; for an end to unjust arrests and imprisonment, torture, and extortion by Pakistani police and other Government officials; for the abolition of the abusive blasphemy laws, and the release of Christian prisoners sentenced to die because of them.

- Please pray for Pakistan's leaders to take a firm stand against the Islamic extremists operating in their midst; that *Shari'a* law is not imposed; that just laws are applied evenly in Pakistan; that the Pakistani Government protects the lives and religious freedoms of its minority citizens, and punish those who persecute them.

- Please pray also that Christians and Western governments and nations avoid any actions, policies or attitudes that might give scandal and thus jeopardize the work or the lives of Christians in Pakistan.

Week Four: The Arab Republic of Egypt

The Spirit Himself bears witness with our spirit that we are children of God, and if children, heirs also, heirs of God and fellow heirs with Christ, if indeed we suffer with Him in order that we may also be glorified with Him. For I consider that the sufferings of this present time are not worthy to be compared with the glory that is to be revealed to us. For the anxious longing of the creation waits eagerly for the revealing of the sons of God (Romans 8: 16-19).

Egypt is located in the lush Nile valley of Northern Africa, and is perhaps best known for its sweeping deserts and towering pyramids. Believers know it as the starting point of the great Exodus, and the land where Mary and Joseph hid the baby Jesus.

Egypt has an ancient Christian tradition, believed to have its origins in the evangelisation of Saint Mark. Today, Egypt is a predominantly Muslim society. Of the Christians that remain, Coptic Orthodox Christians or "Copts" as they are known, comprise about 90 percent. The remaining 10 percent include Protestants, Anglicans, and Catholics. Together they constitute one of the largest Christian communities in the Middle East.

The leader of the Copts is Pope Shenouda III, who a few years ago, met with Pope John Paul II, during one of the latter's visits to the Middle East.

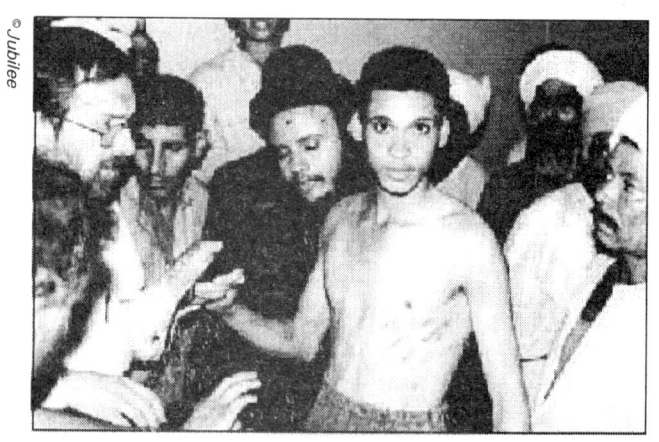

Violence against Christians in Egypt is far too commonplace

Christianity in Egypt has a long history of persecution and discrimination. The first brutal assault there was recorded in the 8th Century, when Umar II and his radical Muslim armies raided Egypt and set out to destroy its Christians. Under "The Pact of Umar" they lost ownership of their land to Muslims, and were forced to pay a land tax called the *kharaj* just to use what was rightfully their own. Their churches were destroyed, and they were forbidden from building new ones or repairing the old. Church bells, crosses, banners, and sacred books were banned, and services had to be conducted in silence.

Christians were ridiculed, forced to wear

discriminatory clothing, and ride on donkeys. Around their necks they were required to carry their "tribute" to Muslims, known as the *jizya*, a mafia-style extortion tax or form of "protection money," which they had to pay Muslims not to kill them. Shocking as it might seem, countless Christians in

Soldiers on patrol outside an Evangelical church in Egypt

Egypt are still forced to pay the *jizya* or face having their homes and businesses burned to the ground, and their families murdered. Even more shocking, is that the widespread imposition of this practice goes utterly ignored by the Government.

Violence against Christians is far too commonplace in Egypt: in the past ten years, there have been more than one hundred and twenty attacks on churches, and more than five hundred attacks on Christian properties and businesses. In 1996, Islamic extremists burned down fifty-six Christian homes in the village of Kafr Demian in just one day.

In August 1998, two Coptic Christians were murdered in the mostly Christian village of Al-Kosheh. Police responded by arresting, detaining, and torturing more than one thousand Christian villagers over the following two months. Those abused include relatives of the victims, women, and children. Human rights organizations have documented horrific physical and psychological torture of these by police, including beatings, whippings, and electric shocks. Finally, a Christian villager was convicted and imprisoned for the murder of the two Copts, despite overwhelming evidence of his innocence.

Two years later, Al-Kosheh was besieged yet again. At the turn of the new millennium, twenty-one Christians were massacred by Muslims, while police stood by. Many were literally hacked to death, while others were murdered execution-style after refusing to renounce their faith. Two hundred and sixty Christian homes and businesses were gutted and looted during the three-day rampage.

Only after an international outcry did the Egyptian authorities arrest some of those responsible. Yet in the end, every single murderer was set free and went unpunished.

In July 2000, Muslim gunmen killed a Christian farmer and wounded five other Christians in Giza because a church was being built there. The following December, a 75-year-old priest was stabbed and seriously wounded by Muslims near Sohag. In February 2002, Muslim villagers firebombed a newly reconstructed church in Minya.

These incidents demonstrate that the Egyptian Government's justice system and security police provide little protection for its Christian citizens. Moreover, the Egyptian Government is responsible for much discrimination and persecution by promoting anti-Christian television programming, making it extremely difficult for Christians to build and repair churches, and even frequently detaining and torturing Muslim converts to Christianity. Egypt even imprisons those who speak out against its horrific human rights abuses, claiming that such revelations "tarnish the image of Egypt."

Prayer Points:

- Please pray for the protection and deliverance of Christians in Egypt; that they will be strengthened in their faith and comforted in their suffering; that God in His mercy will spare them from further unspeakable horror, and raise up intercessors and advocates to lighten their heavy burdens.

- Please pray for an end to the attacks, murders, destruction of homes and churches by Muslims; for an end to unjust arrests and imprisonment, torture, and extortion by Egyptian police and other Government officials; for the release of Christian prisoners and those imprisoned for speaking out against the Government's discriminatory practices against religious and other minorities.

- Please pray that the Government of Egypt will protect the lives and religious freedoms of its minority citizens and bring to justice those who unlawfully persecute them; and that Western governments no longer turn a blind eye to religious persecution of this kind.

- Please pray that Christians in the West, and Western nations and governments avoid scandal and hypocrisy, and do nothing to exacerbate Muslim hatred of Christians in Egypt or elsewhere, thus putting the lives of Christians, church leaders and missionaries at risk; pray also that our churches and societies may be seen as examples of peace, justice and charity.

Week Five:
The Islamic Republic of Iran

Even though I walk through the valley of the shadow of death, I fear no evil; for Thou art with me (Psalm 23:4).

99 percent of Iran's 67 million inhabitants are Muslims. Of the religious minorities making up the remaining percent, only approximately 220,000 are believed to be Christians, over half of those ethnic Orthodox. It is difficult to ascertain the numbers of Christians in the Islamic Republic of Iran, because conversion to Christianity by a Muslim is a crime punishable by death. Meanwhile, Christians who share their faith with Muslims face the constant threat of torture and death.

Islamic religious police from Iran's Ministry of Culture and Islamic Guidance, increasingly threaten, imprison, and torture Christians because of their faith. They have arrested and detained as many as forty at one time and have been responsible for the confirmed deaths of eight others since 1988. Fifteen to twenty-three converts from Islam to Christianity disappeared between November 1997 and November 1998 after their baptisms were discovered by the authorities. It is presumed that most, if not all, have been murdered.

The same fate is believed to have been shared by the victims of three further disappearances in the year 2000. After the arrest of one of these, a convert in Tehran, a friend of his was interrogated about their relationship. On inquiring about the convert's whereabouts, the Government official told him that the Christian was "in hell," clearly indicating he was dead.

Rev. Haik Hovespain was one of several church leaders killled for their faith.

Another of these three, also a Tehran convert, was abducted by Government-sponsored paramilitary vigilantes called "Basijis" and detained for 3 weeks, during which time he was tortured so severely that, when he was finally released, he could no longer speak, write, or walk. After being hospitalized, it was further discovered that this persecuted believer was suffering from internal bleeding.

The third Tehran convert was visited in his apartment by two agents of the Ministry of

Medhi Dibaj was imprisoned for nine years under charges of apostasy, and was killed after his arrest.

Information. Having warned him on two prior occasions to abandon Christianity and stop attending an underground church, the two agents now walked him out of the apartment, produced a rope, and hanged him right there in front of the entrance.

Since President Khatami's 1997 election and 2001 re-election, Iranian police no longer limit arrests to key church leaders. Instead, they focus their threats and intimidation tactics on ordinary Christians and entire house-churches, arresting groups of twenty to forty believers at a time. Evangelical churches have been closed down, Christians are forced to carry membership cards, and members of evangelical congregations are subject to identity checks by authorities posted outside church doors. Pastors have been ordered to report new members to the Government, which they have refused to do at great danger to their own lives.

Political dissent is ruthlessly suppressed - with more that 400 public executions, including the hanging and stoning of women.

A woman's testimony in Iran is worth only half that of a man, making it virtually impossible for women to redress legal grievances. Iranian law allows for the practice of "Siqeh," or temporary marriage. This Shi'a Muslim custom permits single or married Muslim men to take as many "Siqeh" wives as they like. Siqeh "marriages" can last for as short as a single evening or even a single sexual encounter. "Wives" of such "marriages" are not granted rights associated with traditional marriage. Perhaps even more shocking, is that in Iran, girls as young as 9-years-old can be given in marriage to Muslim husbands.

In October 2000, Iran's Parliament passed a bill to raise the legal age of marriage for women from 9 to 15. A month later, the Council of Guardians rejected the bill as contrary to Islamic law. Every year since 1999 then, the United States Secretary of State has designated Iran as a country of particular concern under the International Religious Freedom Act for its particularly severe violations of religious freedom. Although many European governments, including Britain's, continue 'business as usual' with Iran, President George W. Bush has maintained a strong policy towards Iran, describing it as part of an "axis of evil," together with Iraq and North Korea.

Prayer Points:

- Please pray for the protection and deliverance of Christians in the Islamic Republic of Iran; that he will strengthen them in their faith and comfort them in their suffering; that in His mercy he will spare them from further unspeakable horror, and raise up intercessors and advocates to lighten their heavy burdens.

- Please pray for an end to the arrests, detentions, disappearances, torture, maiming, and execution of Christians by Iran's Ministry of Culture and Islamic Guidance and other Government authorities. Please pray for an end to the Government's brutal crackdown against Christian converts, evangelical Christians, and house-church members and leaders.

- Please pray that the Government of Iran will accept the religious diversity of its citizens, protect the lives and religious freedom of its minorities, and that the lives and human rights of women and children in Iran would be respected and protected.

- Please pray also that, in making this plea for the rights and dignity of Iranian women and children, we recognize and vow to end the indignities done to Western women by our Godless culture and the legalized, common slaughter done to millions of unborn children by abortion in the West. May genuine repentance turn our lives to Godliness.

Week Six:
The Kingdom of Saudi Arabia

For to you it has been granted for Christ's sake, not only to believe in Him, but also to suffer for His sake (Philippians 1:29).

Saudi Arabia is an absolute monarchy in which Islam is both the official and the only religion tolerated. All of its 15 million citizens, therefore, must be Muslims. Moreover, "Wahhabism" is the only interpretation of Islamic teaching that is permitted in Saudi Arabia. State-mandated Wahhabism alone is tolerated, and all other types of teachings are prohibited.

Recent international attention has focused on the immense financial support given by the Saudi Government to promote Wahhabism in other countries. This raises troubling questions about the Saudi Government's role in exporting religious intolerance throughout the world.

In addition to restricting the religious freedom of its own citizens, of the 7 million foreigners who reside in Saudi Arabia, those who profess a faith other than Wahhabi Islam live in grave danger, as practice of any other religious faith is strictly prohibited. Foreign missionaries are not permitted in Saudi Arabia. Proselytizing and distribution of any religious literature other than that of Wahhabi Islam is illegal, and foreigners accused of sharing their faith have been arrested, tortured, and deported. Although the Government claims to permit "private" worship, Christians worshipping in their homes have been harassed, arrested, imprisoned, tortured, lashed, and deported by Saudi authorities.

Saudi Arabia's religious police, known as the "Mutawaa," frequently raid Christian services in private homes. They have also harassed, detained, and "punished" individuals who stray from what they deem "appropriate" dress. For example, while protecting Saudi Arabians during the Gulf War, American Chaplains in the US Armed Services were forbidden to wear crosses and other symbols of their faith.

The US Conference of Catholic Bishops estimates that there are five hundred thousand to one million Catholics living in Saudi Arabia. Many are of Filipino descent, and have faced persecution on account of their faith. Two Filipino Catholics were arrested and imprisoned in early 2002 for conducting a prayer-meeting in their home. These two were later sentenced to 150 lashes, imprisoned for 30 days, and afterwards deported. In contrast, two Filipino Christians were beheaded in 1997 for proselytizing.

Saudi Arabia's legal system is based on strict Islamic law called *Shari'a*, by which every person accused of a criminal offence is subject to its often brutal punishments. Conversion to Christianity by a Muslim is punishable by death, and unless the convert recants, he will be executed by Saudi authorities.

Women in Saudi Arabia are considered the property of their male Muslim owners. Muslim men are permitted to marry four women, and may take as many "Al-Mesyar" wives as they like. Al-Mesyar "marriages," much like the Siqeh marriages in Iran, are entered into for the sole purpose of satisfying the Muslim man's sexual desires, and can last for as short as 30 minutes. The man has no legal responsibility to provide for any children born of such unions. All children born to a Muslim man are automatically designated as Muslims, regardless of the mother's religious beliefs or the country in which the child was born or raised. In the case of divorce, the children are removed permanently from the mother's custody at 7 years of age for boys and 9 years of age for girls. The children are then awarded either to the father or to the deceased father's family, and the mother is often prevented from visiting her children after divorce. Cases of abductions of Western children by Saudi fathers have received international attention as the Saudi Arabian Government consistently refuses to return the kidnapped children to their foreign mothers despite the rights and foreign citizenship of the children.

Since the year 2000, the United States Commission on International Religious Freedom has repeatedly recommended to Secretaries of State

Madeline Albright and Colin Powell that Saudi Arabia be designated a country of particular concern under the International Religious Freedom Act for its severe violations of religious freedom. To date, both US Secretaries of State have refused the designation. It is widely believed that human rights concerns are being muted because of the West's "more pressing" interests in appeasing our oil-rich "friend and ally," Saudi Arabia.

Prayer Points:

● Please pray for the protection and deliverance of Christians and other religious minorities in Saudi Arabia; that they will be strengthened in their faith and comforted in their suffering; that God in His mercy will spare them from further unspeakable horror, and raise up intercessors and advocates to lighten their heavy burdens.

● Please pray for an end to the harassment, arrests, deportations, detentions, flogging, and torture of Christians by Saudi Arabia's Mutawaa religious police and other Government authorities. Please pray for an end to the Government's crackdown against Christian converts and house-church members and leaders.

● Please pray for an end to the Saudi Government's massive financial support of Islamic terrorism around the world, that the religious diversity of its own citizens and residents would be tolerated and protected; that the Government of Saudi Arabia will respect and protect the lives and human rights of women and children within its borders, and that children abducted from Western countries will be returned home.

- Please pray that Western governments and other world leaders would cease to be silent over the rampant religious persecution of Christians in Saudi Arabia; that they would have the conviction to place greater value on human lives, human dignity, and religious freedom than on their desire to maintain a "friendly" strategic relationship with an oil-rich power broker in the Middle East.

- Recognising that Christians and Muslims, as well as Jews, are all children of Abraham, and that we are all therefore subject to the same commandments that we love God and love our neighbours as ourselves, we pray that God's Holy Word will prevail in dialogue and that all of our hearts turn in repentance to saving faith. Pray also for the humility and shame to recognise that the conflict between these three great world religions constitutes one of the greatest scandals the world has ever seen.

SECTION II:

Persecution of Christians in Communist Asia

Muslim governments and militant Islamic extremists are not alone in their persecution of the 21st Century Christian Church. Brutal Communist regimes continue to stamp out religious faith of all kinds, and Christians are targeted daily for suppression and elimination.

Week Seven:
The Democratic People's Republic of Korea (North Korea)

So they went on their way from the presence of the Council, rejoicing that they had been considered worthy to suffer shame for His name. And every day, in the temple and from house to house, they kept right on teaching and preaching Jesus as the Christ (Acts 5:41-42).

North Korea has attracted international attention over its programme to develop nuclear weapons of mass destruction. In October 2002, US officials announced this constituted a breach of a 1994 United Nations accord. In November and December 2002, North Korea admitted the allegation, pulled out of a global nuclear arms control treaty, announced that it was resuming its nuclear programme, and ejected U.N. inspectors from the country. In January 2003, it announced that it would resume testing nuclear missiles that have the capacity to strike not just its neighbours like South Korea and Japan but even Hawaii, and probably the coast of California. A month later, it announced that it was reactivating its nuclear facilities.

In addition to the threat North Korea's nuclear weapons pose to its neighbours and the world at large, its brutal laws and practices threaten

Christians living within its own borders, in what was once known as the Jerusalem of Asia.

The country officially known as the Democratic People's Republic of Korea is anything but democratic. Its citizens are firmly and brutally oppressed under the communist dictatorship of Kim Jong II, who, with his Government, stop at nothing to eradicate all belief systems other than the worship of Kim himself and his deceased father, Kim II Sung. Both father and son have made every effort to purge the land of all Christian influence.

North Korea has a population of approximately 21 million. The number of Christian believers is unknown, but is estimated at about only 10,000 Protestants and 4,000 Catholics. In the late 1980s, the Government sent two Roman Catholic men to study religion in Rome, but they returned before being ordained priests. It is still unknown whether any Catholic priests, whose roles are fundamental to the Catholic faith, remain in the country. According to a 2002 South Korean press report, the Catholic community in the North has no priest, but weekly prayer services are held in Pyongyang.

Becoming a Christian in North Korea is a serious crime. When North Korean Christians of any denomination desire to gather together to pray or worship, they do so at tremendous risk to their lives, often in underground "house churches", members of which have been beaten, arrested, and murdered because of their religious beliefs. Many are thrown into labor camps or prison, where they are kept in horrific conditions. Defectors have reported water torture, severe beatings, sexual assault and violation, starvation, and eggregious solitary cells. Up to 1 million people are incarcerated in the gulags of North Korea. Scores of Christians, both young and old, have been killed by North Korean authorities since 1999.

In the last 300 years since a Korean, baptised in China and bearing the name Peter, first brought Christianity to Korea, there have been literally thousands of martyrs.

Christians who dare to evangelize or simply share their faith with others, face harsh penalties, including imprisonment and prolonged detention without charge. They also face horrific torture and execution. Former prisoners who have lived to tell, report that inmates held on account of their Christian religious beliefs were treated far worse than others, and are regarded as insane on account of their belief in God. One former prisoner recounted an instance in which a Christian woman was kicked repeatedly and left with her injuries unattended for days because a guard overheard her praying for a child who was being beaten.

In recent years, the brutal North Korean regime has cracked down particularly on Christians who share their faith and those who have ties to evangelical groups operating across the border with China. People who manage to escape into China are often forcibly returned, a practice known as "refoulment", which is committed in blatant disregard for universal human rights instruments and practices that forbid the returning of refugees to countries where they will be persecuted. Several Christians lost their lives in 2001 on account of such activities and associations. The North Korean Government has further tightened its control and increased punishments at the Chinese border, even increasing the award for information on any person doing missionary work.

On the other side of the border, China itself offers a bounty of approximately one month's salary on the head of each North Korean refugee captured within its borders. A further bounty of approximately ten times that is offered on the head of anyone found providing assistance to these

North Korean refugees being prevented from entering China.

refugees, and this is in addition to both the jail time and fines amounting to a lifetime's wages that will be assessed. Not only does China forcibly return Christians and other refugees to North Korea where they are likely to be tortured and killed, but it also refuses to permit the United Nations High Commission on Refugees (UNHCR) access to refugees in provinces that border on North Korea.

An aerial photograph of Camp 22 at Haengyong in north-eastern North Korea.

China's solution to its refugee "problem" is chillingly reminiscent of Hitler's final solution to the "Jewish problem" — eliminate them. When these refugees are returned to North Korea, many will be deemed to have committed political treason. Some will be executed. Many will face years in political prisoner camps where they will be tortured, and worked and starved until they die.

The refoulement by China of North Korean refugees is committed in direct violation of two important international human rights instruments that China has signed. As signatories to both the *Convention on Refugees* and the *Convention Against Torture*, China has agreed not to refoul refugees to a country where they will be persecuted or tortured. It is of vital importance, therefore, that the Chinese be required to comply with their already existing treaty obligations.

Jubilee Campaign believes that the key is in an existing bilateral treaty between China and the UNHCR, whereby the latter maintains a presence in China. The treaty gives the UNHCR the right to unimpeded access to refugees at all times, but China has denied access to the UNHCR for years, in direct violation of this treaty. To address such a violation, the treaty contains a provision whereby either party may call for binding arbitration of the matter. The problem is that the UNHCR has never initiated arbitration over China's refusal to grant it access to North Korean refugees. Jubilee Campaign is currently leading an effort to compel UNHCR arbitration.

Since the year 2000, the United States Secretary of State has designated North Korea a country of particular concern under the International Religious Freedom Act for its particularly severe violations of religious freedom. Moreover, North Korea is one of only three nations to be designated as part of an "axis of evil" by US President George W. Bush in January 2002.

Prayer Points:

- Please pray for the protection and deliverance of Christians in North Korea; that they will be strengthened in their faith and comforted in their suffering; that God in His mercy will spare them from further unspeakable horror, and raise up intercessors and advocates to lighten their heavy burdens.

- Please pray for an end to the disappearances, arrests, detentions, imprisonment, beatings, torture, and execution of Christians by North Korean authorities, and that the Government will end its brutal crackdown against Christian house-church members and leaders.

- Please pray that the Government of North Korea will tolerate and protect the human rights and religious freedom of it citizens, and that it will cease offering bounties on the heads of refugees who flee from persecution.

- Please pray that the UNHCR will agree to initiate arbitration into the issue of China's refusal to permit access to North Korean refugees; that arbitration will be successful, and that the UNHCR will have unfettered access to North Korean refugees in China. Please pray that China's treaty obligations will be honoured, and that it will no longer refouler North Korean refugees to a country where they face persecution and death.

Week Eight: The People's Republic of China

Consider what I say, for the Lord will give you understanding in everything. Remember Jesus Christ, risen from the dead, descendant of David, according to my gospel, for which I suffer hardship even to imprisonment as a criminal; but the Word of God is not imprisoned. For this reason I endure all things for the sake of those who are chosen, that they also may obtain the salvation which is in Christ Jesus and with it eternal glory (2 Timothy 7-10).

China is the most heavily populated country in the world, with a current population of 1.3 billion people, of whom an estimated 30 to 70 million are Protestants and 13 million Catholics. Only about 15 million Protestants are members of the Government-controlled "Three Self Church," and about 5 million Catholics belong to the Government-controlled churches of the "Chinese Catholic Patriotic Association." The majority of Christians have joined unregistered, and thus illegal, "underground" churches free from Government manipulation.

The Chinese Communist Party, under Mao Zedong, took over Mainland China in 1949 after a bitter and protracted civil war. Since that time, Christianity has been associated with Western imperialism and with the Western forces that supported the rival Kuomintang (KMT), led by Chiang Kai-shek. On coming to power in China, the Communist Party expelled foreign missionaries and clergy, and began a systematic pattern of persecution against the native Chinese Christians left behind. The 1989 events culminating in the Tiananmen Square massacre precipitated increased repression of many activities, including religious practice, which the Chinese Government perceives as a threat. In 1999 the Chinese authorities intensified their crackdown on unregistered religious activities. Some observers believe this is the most destructive campaign against Christians since the period of the Cultural Revolution from 1966 to 1976 when all churches were closed and many Christians were killed for their faith.

This new crackdown has primarily targeted evangelical Christian groups, Protestant house-churches, and the underground Roman Catholic Church, as well as adherents to spiritual groups like Falun Gong, Mentu Hui, and localized Buddhist groups. Church leaders in particular are the frequent targets of harassment, interrogations, detention, and physical abuse including torture. Ordinary church members are also subject to such treatment.

Religious persecution in China takes many forms, including long periods of imprisonment in labour camps; large-scale round-ups of Christians, frequent detention of individuals for questioning, restriction of an individual to a town or village; destruction of church buildings; confiscation of property, and censorship of religious publications. Torture by police is common, and has led to the deaths of many Christians.

One of China's state-controlled "3-Self" churches.

In provinces with large Catholic populations such as Hunan and Hubei, the Government's programme of forced abortion and compulsory sterilization has targeted Catholic families. China's one-child policy gives it the distinction of being the only country in the world where it is illegal to have a brother or sister. From the right to a family to the right to worship freely, the Chinese Communist Party has long exhibited an antagonistic attitude towards Christians.

In the 1950s, Chinese Communists attacked the Roman Catholic Church for its continued loyalty to Rome. The Catholic Patriotic Association was formed and bishops were ordained by the Chinese authorities without Papal permission. To this day, the Chinese Government will not allow the Vatican to appoint bishops. In response, loyal Catholics formed underground churches. As a result, many priests have been imprisoned – some for more than two decades – for refusing to accept a Communist-controlled Church. According to a 2002 US State Department report, there are thought to be some thirty-seven Catholic bishops operating "underground," ten to fifteen of whom may be in prison or under house-arrest.

In Hebei, where an estimated half of the country's Catholics reside, local authorities have been known to force underground priests and believers to choose between joining the official Church or face punishment such as fines, job-loss, detentions, and having their children barred from school. Some Catholics have been forced into hiding. Also in 2002, the authorities detained Catholic underground

Bishop Jia Zhiguo, of Hebei, for several days before the start of Holy Week, in a failed attempt to pressure him to join the Chinese Catholic Patriotic Association. Bishop Su Zhimin, has been missing since his arrest in 1997, despite repeated inquiries from the international community on his status and whereabouts. At least three other underground Catholic bishops remain under detention in Hebei.

Several non-governmental organizations (NGOs), report that a number of Catholic priests and lay leaders have been beaten and abused in recent years, and that many have been arrested and detained for various lengths of time. Bishop Joseph Fan Zhongliang, of Shanghai, remains under surveillance and often has his movements restricted. Bishop Zeng Jingmu, who was released from a labour camp in 1998, was arrested in Jiangxi in September 2000. The Government denies his arrest, and also denies that it is detaining the elderly Bishop Yang Shudao, who was arrested by a large group of police in February 2000. No information has been provided as to his whereabouts or condition. Authorities also detained Bishop Shi Enxiang, on Palm Sunday 2001 in Beijing.

Like their Catholic brothers and sisters, Protestants, particularly evangelicals, have suffered for their faith in China. Protestant house-church leaders Allen Yuan and Wang Mingdao, for instance, spent more than twenty years in a labor camp for their Christian faith. On February 5, 2002, a Xiamen court sentenced three members of an evangelical Protestant preaching team to seven years in prison for "using a cult organization to violate the law".

Pastor Lam, one of China's most well-known independent church leaders, next to the banning order on his church.

In April 2001, seventeen Christians were arrested and accused of leading or being members of a "heretical religious organization" called the South China (Huanan) Church. In December 2001, Pastor Gong Shengliang, his niece, Li Ying, and three others were sentenced to death on a wide range of criminal charges, including rape, arson, and assault.

In October 2002, the Hubei High People's Court overturned the death sentences of Pastor Gong, Li

Ying, and the three others – Xu Fuming, Hu Yong, and Gong Bangkun. They are still in prison, however, awaiting a retrial.

The evidence used to convict Pastor Gong and the others included forced confessions obtained from three young women who are members of the church. In letters written to their families that were later published, the three describe how they were tortured by police until they agreed to sign statements claiming that they had been raped by Pastor Gong.

Zhang Hongjuan explains how police officers at the Public Security Bureau Detention Centre in Zhongxiang City, Hubei Province, shackled her hands and feet, ripped open her shirt, and beat her on her breasts with an electric baton. Li Tongjin describes how police at the same detention centre shackled her hands and feet, ripped open her shirt, and beat her on her breasts and legs with an electric baton.

Yang Tongni describes being kicked, beaten, and whipped by police at the Jingmen Police School and Jingmen No. 1 Detention Centre. Her hands were cuffed behind her back and books wedged between the handcuffs and her back, while she was tied up with ropes. Yang Tongni and Li Tongjin are reported to be serving 3-year terms at a hard-labour "re-education" camp. The whereabouts of Zhang Hongjuan are unknown.

Other persons arrested along with Gong and his

niece were sentenced to prison for periods varying between two years and life. At least fourteen were reportedly arrested while authorities sought Pastor Gong. Many of them were beaten and tortured.

In February 2002, Jubilee Campaign USA, together with the Committee for Investigation on Persecution of Religion in China published a report, entitled *Religion and National Security in China*, which contains translations of secret official Chinese documents that were smuggled out of the country. Relating to the years 1999-2001, these documents clearly outline the Government's intent to repress religious expression outside of Government control, and to use harsh criminal penalties in a systematic effort to eliminate unregistered religious groups.

One such secret document produced by the Department for Public Security in China's Anhui Province and dated March 6, 2001 states: "As China and the Vatican discussed establishing diplomatic relations, the public security bodies in the entire province, together with the United Front and religion department began to search, educate, convert, reconnoitre and control some key members of the underground Catholics".

China's customs officials monitor for the "smuggling" of bibles and other religious materials into the country. On January 28, 2002, Hong Kong resident Li Guangqiang was sentenced to 2 years in prison for smuggling annotated versions of the Bible onto the mainland. Li had been detained in May

2001 and was released in early February 2002 on medical parole after Christian groups and political leaders around the world expressed concern over his detention.

Since 1999, the US Secretary of State has designated China a country of particular concern under the International Religious Freedom Act for particularly severe violations of religious freedom. Yet despite China's blatant and horrific human rights violations, the US Government continues to confer "favoured nation status" upon it.

Great Britain continues to provide official aid which is channeled to the population-control programmes - the "one-child policy" through which women are forcibly aborted and sterilised. Christian families particularly have particularly suffered as a consequence.

In his February 16, 2003 letter to US Secretary of State Colin Powell, Elliot Abrams, Chairman of the US Commission on International Religious Freedom, condemns the fact that in the previous two years, the UNCHR has not even debated the issue of human rights in China, the only nation on the US Commission's list of "countries of particular concern" to receive such little attention for its abuses. According to Abrams, China's religious freedom record "has substantially deteriorated and become even more deplorable" during this time." A US-backed UNCHR resolution condemning China's record would "send the message that it cannot violently, systematically violate the right to freedom of religion or other human rights with impunity as far as its relations with the international community is concerned."

Prayer Points:

- Please pray for the protection and deliverance of Christians in China; that they will be strengthened in their faith and comforted in their suffering. That God in His mercy will spare them from further unspeakable horror, and raise up intercessors and advocates to lighten their heavy burdens.

- Please pray for an end to the disappearances, arrests, interrogations, detentions, imprisonment, beatings, torture, execution, and prolonged "re-education through labour" in Communist death camps, to which Christians are subjected by the Chinese Communist Party; that Chinese authorities will end their brutal crackdown against Christian house-church members and leaders, and cease destroying church buildings and confiscating property, bibles, and religious symbols and literature.

- Please pray that the Government of China will tolerate and protect the human rights and religious freedom of it citizens; that it will abolish its programmes of forced abortion and compulsory sterilization and that it will no longer deprive

Christian children of education, or withhold jobs and food from their parents.

● Please pray for the release of Pastor Gong Shengliang and all Christians and others imprisoned in China on account of their faith. Please pray that Western governments and other world leaders will no longer remain silent with regard to the horrific human rights abuses in China. That China take steps to ensure the human rights of its citizens.

● Please pray that China will cease offering bounties on the heads of North Korean refugees who have crossed its borders, and that the UNHCR will agree to initiate arbitration into the issue of China's refusal to permit access to North Korean refugees; that arbitration will be successful, and that the UNHCR will have unfettered access to North Korean refugees in China. Please pray that China's treaty obligations will be honoured, and that it will no longer refouler North Korean refugees to a country where they face persecution and death.

● Please pray that Christians in Britain will bring pressure on their Government to cease supporting China's "one-child policy".

Week Nine: Vietnam

Fixing our eyes on Jesus, the author and perfector of faith, who for the joy set before Him endured the cross, despising the shame, and has sat down at the right hand of the throne of God. For consider Him who has endured such hostility by sinners against Himself, so that you may not grow weary and lose heart (Hebrews 12:2-3).

Vietnam is a country of approximately 80 million people, ruled by the Communist Party of Vietnam (CPV). An estimated 6 to 7 million Roman Catholics live there and an estimated 1 million, more than half of whom belong to unregistered evangelical "house-churches."

The death in September 2002 of Cardinal Francois Xavier Nguyen Van Thuan, who spent thirteen years in Communist prisons, nine of those in solitary confinement, reminds us of the price Christians have paid for their faith. Persecution of Christians has continued since the Communists took control of South Vietnam in 1975.

Vietnamese security forces often employ martial law, beatings, and teargas in a systematic attempt to eliminate the Christian faith. One common practice is to force Christians to renounce their faith. Reports of this practice have increased in recent years, particularly as it is applied against Hmong Protestant Christians in several northwestern villages, and Montagnards (also known as the Degar people), of the Central Highlands. Officials there have also demolished churches, detained, beaten, harassed

Christian communities have come under increasing pressure from the Vietnamese authorities.

people, and extorted goods, livestock, and money from Protestant believers. In April 2002, officials cut off electricity to the homes of ethnic Ede villagers in the Phu Yen Province after they refused to renounce Christianity. Members of Hmong and

Montagnard Christian populations have also been charged with "practising religion illegally". Authorities frequently invoke provisions of the penal code that allow for jail terms of up to three years for "abusing freedom of speech, press, or religion".

At a Government conference in 2001, the CPV reportedly made clear its goal to eliminate Christianity among the Hmong tribes people before its follow-up conference in 2005. Many Hmong Christian leaders have fled their villages and now live in the forest or in caves to escape the religious persecution directed against them. At least twenty Hmong pastors have been imprisoned in Vietnam for their Christian faith.

On December 29, 2002, police used noxious gas to break up a Christian worship gathering attended by forty Hmong believers in Dien Bien Dong. Twenty were hospitalized, and the hospital was surrounded by police, apparently to prevent their escape after release.

The Montagnards are indigenous hill tribes comprising over thirty tribal groups of an estimated six hundred thousand people based in the Central Highlands. About four thousand of these are Christians, both Protestant and Catholic. Communist authorities have singled out Montagnards for persecution both because they assisted the US Army during the Vietnam War, and because of their Christian faith.

In December 2001, police in Buon Cuor Knia

village in Dak Lak Province beat and shocked with electric wires twelve Christians who were being punished for having attempted to flee across the border to Cambodia. Those who manage to escape are often subjected to even worse abuse. On December 28, 2001, Cambodian authorities deported at least one hundred and sixty-seven Montagnard refugees who had fled from persecution in Vietnam. After being forcibly returned to their country of persecution, they were detained by Vietnamese authorities who tortured many of them.

One horrific example is that of H'Boc Eban. She and her three children fled to Cambodia, but were subsequently deported to Vietnam. H'Boc was severely tortured by Vietnamese officials who forced electric cattle prods into her mouth so many times that she finally lost consciousness and had to be hospitalized. The fate of her three children is unknown.

The Montagnard human rights organization, The Montagnard Foundation, reports: "Today the devastation continues and we are faced with continued and sustained policies that exploit our homelands and persecute our race through forced assimilation, human rights violations and genocide enacted by the current Vietnamese Government". In fact, three Montagnard Christians were executed by lethal injection on October 29, 2002. Y-Suon Mlo, Y-Het Nie Kdam, and Y-Wan Ayun were arrested after taking part in a peaceful demonstration in

February 2001 to protest against the arrest and torture of two other Montagnard Christians.

Catholic Father Nguyen Van Ly initiated a campaign for religious freedom in Vietnam in 2000.

Fr Van Ly is serving a 15-year sentence for speaking out for religious freedom and social change

He later testified before a US Congressional committee, urging Congress to postpone the ratification of a bilateral trade agreement with Vietnam as long as religious restrictions persisted. He was critical of both the Communist Government's abuse of religious freedom, and the one-party system itself.

As a result, police surrounded his church in February 2001 and placed him under administrative probation. His detention was reported widely in the state-controlled press, which identified him as a "traitor" for criticizing the Government. The following May, hundreds of police officers again surrounded his church as he was preparing for Mass, and arrested him. At his trial six months later, he was convicted and sentenced to 15 years in prison for, among other things, "damaging the Government's unity policy." In 2003, a Jubilee delegation, led by Congressman Joseph Pitts (Republican – Pennsylvania) and Lord Alton, urged the authorities in Hanoi to release Fr Van Ly.

Following that trip, Jubilee established a campaign for Fr Ly's freedom. In July 2003, the Vietnamese authorities reduced Fr Ly's jail sentence from 15 years to 10 years followed by 5 years of house arrest. This is a step in the right direction and is an indication that the authorities are susceptible to international pressure.

Even Christian schoolchildren are subjected to persecution in Vietnam. In March 2001, teachers at a public primary school in Ban Don district ordered all the Christian students to renounce Christ. Those who refused were suspended, and it is unknown whether they have ever been permitted to return to school. It is also reported that Dak Lak authorities prohibit Protestant children from attending school past the third grade. Montagnard children, deprived of their education by authorities, have been further subjected to forced renunciation of Christianity, along with the drinking of pig's blood, an ancient religious ritual of their pre-Christian ancestors.

On many occasions, Hmong Protestant Christians have been pressured by local officials to recant their faith, and forced to perform ancient Hmong religious rituals such as drinking blood from sacrificed chickens mixed with rice wine. The CPV's "Programme 184" was designed specifically to reverse the spread of Protestant Christianity in areas where it has been advancing rapidly. Local and provincial officials in these areas circulated official documents urging people to renounce their illegal "foreign" religion, and to practise animist beliefs, tribal religions, and ancestor worship instead. Christians also suffer from the official "one-child" population policy.

In October 2002, the US Secretary of State designated Vietnam a country of particular concern under the International Religious Freedom Act, for particularly severe violationsof religious freedom.

Prayer Points:

- Please pray for the protection and deliverance of Christians in Vietnam, that they will be strengthened in their faith and comforted in their suffering; that God in His mercy will spare them from further unspeakable horror, and raise up intercessors and advocates to lighten their heavy burdens.

- Please pray for an end to martial law, teargas raids, arrests, interrogations, disappearances, detentions, beatings, torture, imprisonment, and executions of Christians by Vietnamese authorities; that they Government will end their brutal crackdown against Christian house-church members and leaders, and cease its demolition of churches, and extortion of goods, livestock, and money from believers. Please pray also for the release of Fr Van Ly.

- Please pray that the Government of Vietnam will tolerate and protect the human rights and religious freedom of it citizens; that it will no longer employ the abhorrent policies of forcing Christian adults and children to renounce their faith and participate in ancient blood-drinking rituals, and that Christian children will no longer be deprived of an education.

Week Ten:
Laos

He who overcomes shall thus be clothed in white garments; and I will not erase his name from the book of life, and I will confess his name before My Father, and before His angels (Revelation 3:5).

Despite its misleading name, the Lao People's Democratic Republic is ruled by a brutal Communist Government. Laos is a landlocked country wedged between Thailand and Vietnam. It suffered great economic hardship during the Vietnam War and its aftermath, and is today one of the poorest countries in Southeast Asia. The estimated population of Laos is 5.2 million, with approximately 60 to 65 percent Theravada Buddhists, 30 percent animists, and a small Catholic and Protestant Christian minority of approximately 2 percent.

The Roman Catholic Church in Laos is comprised of approximately 30,000 to 40,000 members. Many are ethnic Vietnamese, concentrated in major urban areas along the Mekong River. The Catholic Church is unable to operate effectively in the Highlands and much of the north because churches are not permitted to register, and worship services are restricted. There are approximately 250 to 300 Protestant congregations throughout the country, and Protestant Christians are estimated at 60,000.

Since 1998, the Communist Government has employed brutal and systematic tactics to rid the country of Christians, and Protestants in Laos have been targeted with particular severity. In 1999, the Communist regime declared Christianity "the

One of the few evangelical pastors in Laos.

number one enemy of the State", viewing it as an "imperialist foreign religion" that is backed by political interests in the West, particularly the United States. Believers arrested for their religious activities in Laos have been charged with exaggerated security or other criminal offences. Once arrested, a "religious offender" can be held indefinitely without trial, and has virtually no protection under the law.

In one all too typical case, a Christian leader named Pa Tood, was detained in 1999 in Savannakhet City Jail. He was offered bail on the condition that he renounce his Christian faith, which he refused to do. As punishment, he was placed in solitary confinement, where wooden stocks alternately held his right leg then his left for 24 hours a day. Mr. Tood's legs became swollen, and his health severely deteriorated. He was often deprived of food for several days at a time. His wife, Koom, was arrested with her infant child on March 17, 1999, and both were deprived of food in jail. Koom had a nervous breakdown after seven days in prison, and was eventually released.

In April 2002, eleven Christian citizens were arrested in Bokeo Province when they re-entered Laos from Thailand with religious material. All eleven were required to pay fines before finally being released.

Another strategy implemented by the Communist Government has been its effort to force Christians to renounce their faith. The Lao Evangelical Church (LEC) has been specifically targeted on account of its rapid growth over the last decade, its contact with religious groups abroad, the active proselytizing on the part of some members, and its independence of central "government" controls. Officials in some areas of Vientiane, Luang Prabang, and Savannakhet provinces forced LEC Christians to sign renunciations of their faith under threat of arrest, denial of educational opportunity for their children, and restrictions on access to Government services. Some detainees held for their religious beliefs were released only after they agreed to renounce Christianity. Some civil servants were threatened with loss of their positions if they did not sign renunciations of their faith. In November 2001,

Congressman Pitts (left) and Lord Alton (right) raise religious liberties issues with a Laos Government minister

a prominent LEC pastor was shot and killed near his home in Sayaboury.

LEC members and leaders are subjected also to arrest, detention, and imprisonment for their religious activities in Laos. In March 2002, authorities in Savannakhet arrested and detained two pastors who were presiding at a funeral. Both were detained for several weeks before being released. Two months later, Somsaad village officials in the same province detained twenty Christians who were attending a Sunday morning worship service. They were accused of holding an unauthorized meeting and taken to the district office where all twenty were detained for several weeks before being released. On the same day, three church leaders were arrested in Dongphoum village for conducting an unauthorized worship service. The three were manacled in a jail cell, where they are believed to remain today.

Other Christians have also been arrested and detained for their religious activities. In June 2002, four ethnic Yao were arrested in Luang Namtha Province for holding an unauthorized prayer service. All four were manacled in their cells, and are believed to be there still. That same month, in Kasi district of Vientiane Province, two ethnic Khmu church leaders were arrested for conducting an "unauthorized" prayer service at the home of a sick church member. Both have since been detained.

Three Catholic churches and a school have been seized by the Communist authorities and never returned; bishops have spent time in jail, and catechists need more resources to undertake evangelisation.

In October 2002, the US Secretary of State designated Laos a country of particular concern under the International Religious Freedom Act, for particularly severe violations of religious freedom. In its International Religious Freedom Report released the same month, the US State Department observed: "The Government's tolerance of religionvaried by region and by religion, with Christian Protestants continuing to be the target of most harassment."

Despite its oppressive history, Laos has taken some positive steps in the area of religious freedom. In the summer of 2002, prison gates in Laos were literally thrown open to many Christians who were imprisoned for their faith. The Laotian government passed laws that summer which give official recognition to the Lao Evangelical Churches (LEC). We thank God for this unprecedented turn of events. As we engage consistently at a political and economic level on behalf of those who suffer for their faith, it is encouraging to know that such efforts can eventually bring progress. Only time will tell if the implementation of these new laws will bring true religious freedom, or simply more "authorized" religious groups under Gvernment control.

There are still at least 19 religious prisoners and detainees in Laos, all of them Christians. Many have been singled out for mistreatment while in confinement, and have suffered as a result of inadequate food rations, lack of medical care, and cramped quarters. Our prayers are still desperately needed, as is our activism on behalf of those who continue to suffer in silence.

Prayer Points:

- Please pray for the protection and deliverance of Christians in Laos; that they will be strengthened in their faith and comforted in their suffering; that God in His mercy will spare them from further unspeakable horror, and raise up intercessors and advocates to lighten their heavy burdens.

- Please pray for an end to the arrests, interrogations, disappearances, detentions, beatings, torture, imprisonment, and executions of Christians by authorities in Laos; that Laos' Communist Government would end its brutal crackdown against Christian house-church members and leaders, and cease its abhorrent policy of forcing Christians to renounce their faith under threat of arrest, loss of employment, denial of education for their children, and access to Government services, and return confiscated churches and schools.

- Please pray that the Government of Laos will respect and protect the human rights and religious freedom of it citizens, and that it will release all remaining Christians who are still in prison for their faith.

- Please pray for Christian leaders and missionaries in Laos that they are not compromised by any perceived association with any Western political interests, and that neither their lives nor their work are threatened as a result.

SECTION III:

Persecution of Christians in India, Burma/Myanmar, and in Turkmenistan and the Other Successor States of the Former Soviet Union

Although much of the religious persecution in the world today occurs in countries controlled by either Communist regimes or Islamic governments and extremist groups, these are not alone. In the countries described in the following section, Christians suffer persecution at the hands of Hindu Nationalists (India), Militant Buddhists (Burma/Myanmar), and the governments of relatively new republics still recovering from years of Stalinist domination (Turkmenistan and the successor states of the former Soviet Union).

Week Eleven: India

These things I have spoken to you, that in Me you may have peace. In the world you have tribulation, but take courage; I have overcome the world (John 16:33).

St. Thomas is credited with first introducing Christianity to India, which was also home to the great missionary work of St Francis Xavier, a Jesuit Priest, and of Nobel Prize winner, Mother Theresa, forever remembered for her love and devotion to the "poorest of the poor" in Calcutta and elsewhere. Despite its rich Christian heritage, believers in India today face great persecution and suffering.

More than 82 percent of India's population are Hindu. Approximately 12.5 percent are Muslim, and just over 2 percent are members of India's Christian minority. India employs a centuries old "caste system," by which the rights and standard of living of its citizens are immutably determined at birth. India's Christians, as well as its Muslims and Sikhs, have historically rejected the concept of caste, though many of them are descended from low-caste Hindu families, and continue to suffer the same social and economic limitations as low-caste Hindus.

Since the Bharatiya Janata Party (the BJP), and its allies came to power in India in 1998, it has launched an extremist form of Hindu nationalism called "Hindutva," to purge the country of religious minorities. The BJP has succeeded in portraying Christianity as a suspect "foreign religion"; has passed legislation to effectively limit the rights and activities of Christians in some Indian States including prostelization, and has even rewritten the nation's history books. Religious minorities are now slanderously mischaracterized to India's more than 1.2 million schoolchildren.

In fact, Government officials are trying to make being Hindu synonymous with being Indian. They advocate the Indianization of Islam and Christianity, and say that Catholics "should sever their links with the Pope" – despite the fact that the Catholic Church in India is 2000 years old.

Upper-caste Hindu groups like the BJP fear that Christians may try to convert large numbers of lower-caste Hindus. As this could destroy the rigid caste-hierarchy, the BJP has targeted Christians with a vengeance. In October 2002, the southern state of Tamil Nadu passed a controversial new law banning religious conversion through "coercion or material inducement." Following close on its heals, in March 2003, the Parliament of Gujarat state passed its own anti-conversion bill that requires anyone wanting to convert from one faith to another to get prior permission from a district magistrate. Even for those who convert without threats or inducement, failure to get approval beforehand can result in imprisonment for a year and a small fine. Christians in India fear that these laws will spread countrywide and be easily abused against those who convert to Christianity for any reason.

Christians in Gujarat State share about the persecution they have experienced

Violent attacks against Christians have dramatically increased since the BJP came to power. The central Government has done virtually nothing to stop it or punish the perpetrators. In scores of violent incidents that began to escalate in the summer of 1998, priests and missionaries have been murdered; nuns have been raped and assaulted; churches have been bombed, and Christian converts and parishioners have been intimidated and harassed.

In September 1998 six nuns were raped in a Navapeda convent. The following year, an Australian missionary known for his work with lepers, Graham

Stanes and his two young sons were burned alive in their car. In May 2000, at least thirty people were injured by a bomb explosion during a Christian religious meeting in Machlipatnam. Two months later, a Jesuit priest was attacked and killed while riding home on his motorcycle in South Bihar. In December 2000, a Catholic priest was attacked and killed in Manipur.

2002 saw its share of violence against Christians in India. In February, about seventy men wearing saffron headbands – an emblem of Hindu nationalists – attacked a church near Mysore, in South India, where children were attending a catechism class. About twenty people were seriously wounded. During Christmas Midnight Mass in Maliappota, in West Bengal, a Catholic priest and fourteen others were injured when more than fifty armed men stormed the church. More than one thousand worshippers were assembled when the intruders threw bombs and fired gunshots. Fortunately the attackers fled when police arrived and opened fire.

In January 2003, American missionary, Joseph William Cooper, was wounded when he and seven others were attacked by Hindu nationalists after leaving a church gathering on the outskirts of Trivandrum. He underwent surgery for a deep cut on his right hand. After being released from hospital, he was ordered to leave India within a week for "preaching illegally".

On September 30, 2002, the United States Commission on International Religious Freedom recommended to the US Secretary of State, that India be designated as a country of particular concern under the International Religious Freedom Act for its severe violations of religious freedom.

Prayer Points:

- Please pray for the protection and deliverance of Christians in India; that they will be strengthened in their faith and comforted in their suffering; that God in His mercy will spare them from further unspeakable horror, and raise up intercessors and advocates to lighten their heavy burdens.

- Please pray for an end to the escalating violence being directed against priests, nuns, and Christian congregations. Please pray for an end to the bombings, attacks, intimidation and harassment, rapes, murders, and destruction of homes and churches by militant Hindu nationalists.

- Please pray for the abolition of recent laws aimed at silencing Christians, and punishing those who convert, those who evangelize, and those who believe. Please pray that India's leaders take a firm stand against the extremist Hindu nationalism that is destroying their country, and that India's Government will protect the lives and religious freedoms of its minority citizens, and punish those who persecute them.

Week Twelve: Burma/Myanmar

Blessed is a man who perseveres under trial; for once he has been approved, he will receive the crown of life, which the Lord has promised to those who love Him (James 1:12).

Burma, also known as Myanmar, is a largely rural, densely forested country situated between India and Thailand. Despite its rich culture of ethnic diversity, Burma is ruled by a racist military junta. This brutal regime perpetuates political and economic domination by violently persecuting minority ethnic groups and has turned the ethnic Karin State into one vast concentration camp.

This regime regularly and systematically commits gross violations of human rights, including the forcible relocation of civilians and the widespread use of forced labour, which includes children. Burma's military ruler, General Than Shwe, is a decorated specialist in psychological warfare, and is committed to the imposition of Buddhism upon all citizens of Burma. Reporting on the situation in 1997, the United Nations Special Rapporteur found: "There is essentially no freedom of thought, opinion, expression, or association in Myanmar".

According to Government statistics, nearly 90 percent of Burma's 50 million persons practice

Buddhism, while only 4 percent are Christians (predominantly Baptists, as well as a wide variety of Protestant groups and significant numbers of Catholics). Christianity is the dominant religion among the Kachin ethnic group in the North, and the Chin and Naga ethnic groups in the West. Christianity is also practiced widely among the Karen and Karenni ethnic groups of the southern and eastern regions. As a result, these ethnic groups have been targeted for overt religious persecution by the Burmese military.

The military has pressured Chin Christians to convert to Buddhism by targeting them specifically for forced labour and other abuses of human rights. Since the early 1990s, security forces have torn down, and forced Chin Christian villagers to tear down crosses they have erected in their villages. The villagers are then forced to build Buddhist pagodas to take the place of the crosses. Military units have repeatedly established their camps on the sites of Christian churches and graveyards, which they desecrated and destroyed in the process.

The Burmese military prevents evangelists from preaching in Chin, and soldiers have beaten Christian clergy who refuse to sign statements promising to stop preaching to non-Christians. All gatherings of five or more people are illegal, and families must register all houseguests with the Government. In April 2002, two Chin pastors and their families were arrested in a suburb of Rangoon for having unregistered overnight guests in their homes. The pastors were later transferred to Insein prison (where Aung San Suu Kyi was also imprisoned by the military in 2003), and the status of their eight family members is unknown.

Many Christian Chin are pressured, and some are forced to attend schools for monks and Buddhist monasteries, and are then encouraged to convert to Buddhism. Local Government officials have separated many children of Chin Christians from their parents under the false pretence of giving them free secular education and allowing them to practise

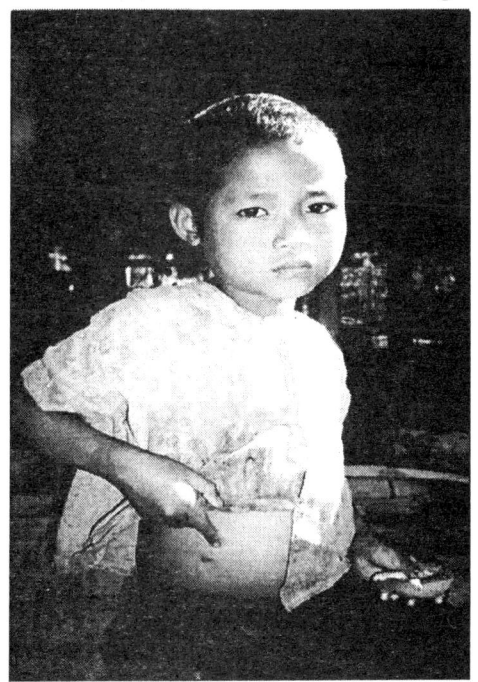

©Jubilee

This 8-year-old girl carried a bullet inside her after being shot by the Burmese Military.

©Jubilee

The Junta's 'scorched earth campaign' has displaced thousands of ethnic minorities people from their homes – © Jubilee

their own religion. In reality, the children were housed in Buddhist monasteries where they were indoctrinated in and converted to Buddhism without their parents' knowledge or consent.

The Chin are not alone in their suffering. In 2001, authorities closed down at least eighty house churches in Rangoon, the capital of Burma, because they did not have proper authorization to hold religious meetings. The Government makes it virtually impossible to obtain official permission to construct or repair "authorized" church buildings, many of which are dilapidated, so this policy effectively closes down all places of Christian worship. Burmese authorities also closed down two Christian homes for children near Rangoon. At least seventeen Christian clergymen were forced into hiding, and five missionaries were ordered to leave the country.

When it comes to human carnage, none have suffered more than Burma's Karen, Karenni and Shan ethnic minorities. These have been subjected to ruthless systematic atrocities that amount to no less than genocide. An estimated 130,000 Karen refugees, many Christians, are festering in camps along the Burma-Thai border, while estimates of 600,000 internally displaced citizens suffer grievously.

Although much of the persecution is ethnically motivated, there are also strong elements of anti-Christian persecution in the Burmese military attacks against Karen and Karenni civilians. With an estimated 8 million people, the Karen are Burma's largest ethnic minority, about 40 percent of whom are Christians. Of the smaller Karenni ethnic group, about 50 percent are Christians, largely as a result of US and British missionary activity in Burma during the 19th century. As a direct result of Burmese military action, more than 350,000 Karen have been internally displaced. Left with little or no food or medicine, they are routinely murdered on sight when discovered by Burmese troops.

Although Karen and Karenni of all religions have been targeted on account of their ethnicity, the Burmese military is especially hostile toward Christians. Soldiers have destroyed numerous churches and killed several pastors. One horrific example is the execution-style massacre of ten Karen villagers, including a pastor and the village headman, in the Karen village of Mukwa.

Karen, Karenni and Shan villagers are also subject to forced labour, systematic destruction of villages, forced relocations, widespread and persistent torture, rape, and murder by Burmese military troops, who make no distinction between adults and children in their campaign of brutal inhumanity. For instance, Burmese soldiers found a little boy and girl aged 3 and 2 respectively, walking around their village crying after the other inhabitants had fled a military shelling attack in 1999. The barbaric troops threw little Saw Ta Plah Plah and

Naw Mi Mu Wah into their house, which was already on fire, and burned the two young children alive.

One young Catholic named James Mawdsley, felt so repelled by the policies being pursued by the Burmese military, that he entered Burma. There he hoped to raise the plight of the Karen and other ethnic Burmese, and to support Aung San Suu Kyi, the opposition leader and Nobel Peace Prize winner who was democratically elected but has spent more than ten years under house arrest by the Burmese military. For this act of bravery and defiance, James was sentenced to seventeen years imprisonment, and spent fourteen months in solitary confinement before he was finally released following international pressure led by the Jubilee Campaign. Jubilee is working with Sister Love – a nun providing refuge for Karen children, with "the Jungle Priest" who runs an illegal school, with a pastor who operates a Bible school and with James Mawdsley's initiative in establishing some small schools on the Burma border.

Since 1999, the US Secretary of State has designated Burma a country of particular concern under the International Religious Freedom Act for particularly severe violations of religious freedom.

Prayer Points:

- Please pray for the protection and deliverance of Christians and other religious and ethnic minorities in Burma/Myanmar; that they will be strengthened in their faith and comforted in their suffering; that God in His mercy will spare them from further unspeakable horror, and raise up intercessors and advocates to lighten their heavy burdens.

- Please pray for an end to the systematic persecution of Christians by Burma's brutal military regime; to the massive forced internal displacement and subhuman living conditions of the displaced; to the destruction of Christian churches and villages, and the military using Christians as forced labor, and for an end to the forced conversion of Christian children to Buddhism.

- Please pray for an end to the barbaric torture, rape, and murder of Christian villagers by Burmese military troops; that the Government of Burma will abandon its genocidal strategy, and begin to respect and protect the human rights and religious freedom of its minority citizens.

- Please pray for those who are working with the Karen and other ethnic minorities, that they are given all possible support by Western nations and by Thailand which has recently taken hostile steps towards the refugees on its border. Pray too that those in the West who have commercial interests in Burma, especially in its oil use those interests to the benefit of its people, and not in even tacit support of Burma's brutal military regime.

Week Thirteen: Turkmenistan and the Successor States of the Former Soviet Union

> *For just as the sufferings of Christ are ours in abundance, so also our comfort is abundant through Christ* (2 Corinthians 1:5).

The fall of the Soviet Union in 1989 did not spell the end of religious repression in Russia and Central Asia. A trend of suppression of religious expression has spread across the successor states of the former Soviet Union.

In 1997, the Russian Government passed a law regarding religion that requires registration of religious groups, and the limitation of recognition of such groups to those who meet arbitrarily established guidelines. The city Government of Moscow even attempted to disband the Salvation Army, labeling it a "dangerous anti-Russian military organization". Thankfully the case was lost and the Salvation Army remains intact in Russia.

In August 2002, Pope John Paul II raised the official status of the Catholic Church in Russia from apostolic administration to full dioceses. This action unleashed a widespread attack. Catholic bishops and priests have been deported, former church-owned property has been turned into brothels, and the state-run media has gone so far as to accuse Franciscans

©Jubilee

This secret Mass was conducted illegally in the Ukraine on Christmas Day during the communist era

in Russia of operating such brothels. The Vatican has requested that Russian President Putin provide an explanation with regard to the deportations.

Andrew Okhotin, a 28-year-old American humanitarian and Harvard divinity student, had participated in the Jubilee Campaign video series episode highlighting the Former Soviet Union. Following his arrival in Moscow on 29 March 2003, Andrew experienced the same persecution suffered by so many of the people he has supported over the years through charitable donations of food, clothing, and money and suffered by his father in the 1980s. Okhotin, who traveled to Russia to deliver charitable contributions to more than 100 needy Christian Russian families (including intended for Shagaldy Atikov's family described below), was confronted by customs officials with the choice of either paying up to $15,000 in bribes or being charged with smuggling contraband currency. Andrew refused to succumb to extortion, and he has been paying for his refusal with his freedom, including four months house arrest and facing up to five years in a foreign prison

In Belarus, a law passed by Parliament continues the trend of legislative attacks on religious freedom. Like its Russian equivalent, the Belarus law calls for registration of religious groups; does not allow prayer groups to meet in private homes; requires Government approval for the publication of any religious materials, and criminalizes evangelism. The

Belarus Government has gone so far as to bulldoze independent Orthodox union churches that are not aligned with the official Belarus Orthodox Church. Subsequently, the Government denied access to diplomats and journalists wishing to inspect the bulldozed sites.

In Kazakhstan and Uzbekistan, some Christian communities have been allowed to register with the State, but most Christians, along with Muslims, Jehovah's Witnesses and other religious adherents there still face many deprivations.

The war between neighboring republics Azerbaijan and Armenia, has led to a staggering one million Azeri refugees. Religious liberties in Azerbaijan have improved since Stalin destroyed the Protestant and Catholic churches, but it has a long way to go in building a truly free civil society. For example, in January 2002, authorities arrested two ethnic Azeri worshippers at a small Pentecostal church in the city of Sumgait during a prayer meeting, and sentenced them to fifteen days imprisonment on charges of hooliganism. The following month, Sumgait police charged and convicted three local Baptists for distributing bibles on the street, and sentenced them to short prison terms. One of these, Rauf Gurbanov, was beaten severely.

Of all the former Soviet republics, Turkmenistan has the most repressive policies toward religion, and is among the most totalitarian states in the world today. Turkmenistan, located on the Caspian Sea between Kazakhstan and Iran, is the North Korea of Central Asia. The ruling regime of authoritarian President Saparmurat Niyazov, is terrifyingly reminiscent of Joseph Stalin's.

Only the official, Soviet-era Sunni Muslim board and the Russian Orthodox Church are recognized by the State as legal religious communities in Turkmenistan. Ethnic Turkmen who have converted to Christianity have been subjected to official harassment and mistreatment. While foreign Christians are deported, ethnic Christians and members of other "illegal unregistered communities," have been detained, imprisoned, harassed, fined, and forced to flee. Their religious services have been disrupted, their congregations dispersed, their religious literature confiscated, and their places of worship bulldozed and destroyed. Some of the unfortunate souls who have not escaped have been tortured, arrested, beaten, imprisoned, and denied food and water for days on end.

In May 2002, a group of Christians in Deinau, Turkmenistan were forced to renounce their faith publicly. They were also forced to swear an oath on a copy of *Rukhnama* (President Niyazov's three-volume spiritual guidebook on Turkmen culture and heritage). Three Christians who refused to renounce Jesus and the Bible were expelled from the village.

Turkmenistan's security police have changed their name from the "KGB" to the "KNB." KNB officials regularly break up religious meetings in private homes, search homes without warrants, confiscate religious literature, and detain and threaten congregants with criminal prosecution and deportation. Even family members of detained religious leaders have been subjected to harassment and internal exile.

Baptists have been singled out for especially severe treatment. One Baptist Pastor, Shagildy Atakov, languished in prison from 1999 to 2002, when he was finally released as a result of persistent international outcry by Jubilee Campaign and others. He remains under house scrutiny.

In November 2000, four ethnic Turkmen Baptists were detained, interrogated and tortured by KNB officials in Anau, after local police found Christian literature and Jesus Films in their car. The KNB harassed and detained the same four Baptists one month later, and three of them were forced to sign documents ceding their houses to the government.

Baptist leaders who do not have Turkmen citizenship, regardless of their legal status in Turkmenistan, are routinely deported to Russia or Ukraine, together with their families and congregants. In July 2001, two Armenian Baptists were deported from Turkmenbashi because of their religious activity. In October 2001, their families were also deported.

In December 2001, an elderly, blind Baptist

woman was threatened with eviction from her apartment in Khazar after holding a Baptist service that had been raided by secret police earlier in the week. Also in 2001, a small Protestant congregation made up of seven adults and four small children fled Turkmenistan on account of religious persecution. The young pastor suffered from a damaged eye, torn eardrum, and other injuries inflicted after secret police found members of his congregation in possession of outlawed Turkmen videos of "The Jesus Film". One of his congregants suffered severe damage to both his eardrums during the beatings, and another developed ongoing heart problems.

Over the last several years, the United States Commission on International Religious Freedom has repeatedly recommended to US Secretaries of State Madeline Albright and Colin Powell that Turkmenistan be designated a country of particular concern under the International Religious Freedom Act for its particularly severe violations of religious freedom.

Throughout the former Soviet Union, from Chechnya and Georgia to Turkmenistan and Belarus, the transition from Communist totalitarianism to societies where basic religious and political freedoms are guaranteed remains an enormous challenge.

Prayer Points:

- Please pray for the protection and deliverance of Christians throughout the former Soviet Union;

that they will be strengthened in their faith and comforted in their suffering; that God in His mercy will spare them from further unspeakable horror, and raise up intercessors and advocates to lighten their heavy burdens.

- Please pray particularly for Turkmenistan's Christians; for an end to the Government's official policy against Christians, which includes harassment, detention, arrests, beatings, torture, deportation, imprisonment, denial of food and water, and forced renunciation of faith, in addition to raiding and destroying private homes, and confiscating religious literature.

- Please pray that Turkmenistan's Government will cease its crackdown against Christian house-church members and leaders, and release those who have been imprisoned for their faith.

- Please pray too, that each successor state of the former Soviet Union will respect and protect the human rights and religious freedom of its citizens.

FINAL NOTES:

A Wake Up Call!

Our first 13-week journey is now complete. We hope that you found it enlightening and inspiring. The Christians we have learned about are not alone in their struggle. As their brothers and sisters, there is always something we can do to help. We are all part of "the household of the faith". Too often we are like the Gethsemane Christians – the ones who fell asleep when their Lord asked for their help. We need to wake up. We can educate. We can advocate. We can pray, and we can give.

The writer of Hebrews exhorts:

> *Remember those in prison as if you were their fellow prisoners, and those who are mistreated as if you yourselves were suffering* (Hebrews 13:3).

In considering the suffering of these "fellow prisoners", there is a danger that we condemn their persecutors. Remember Jesus' reaction to his persecutors, when he was left alone to his agony on the Cross: "Forgive them Father, for they know not what they do" (*Luke 23: 23-24*). Let us pray, therefore, for today's persecutors of his disciples.

We may ask God for relief from suffering of those for whom we have prayed in these meditations, but must trust that God will provide for them in his own way. We may ask that the chalice of suffering be removed, but in the end we must submit with Jesus to the will of his Father: "Let not my will but thine be done".

TAKE ACTION!

If you would like to learn more about the persecution of Christians in a particular country or worldwide, or if you would like to financially support the ongoing efforts of Jubilee Campaign in this regard, please contact us online at www.jubileecampaign.co.uk, or by mail at:

Jubilee Campaign
St Johns, Cranleigh Road
Wonersh, Guildford
GU5 0QX
United Kingdom

You may also contact Jubilee Campaign, USA at the following website and address:

www.jubileecampaign.org

Jubilee Campaign
9689-C Main Street
Fairfax, Virginia 22031
USA

You may wish to purchase copies of the videos that accompany this booklet and which tell the story, country by country. Please consider showing these to friends and urging others to take up the cause of the Suffering Church.

Jubilee